D1329984

Flux

Cynthia Hogue

New Issues Poetry & Prose

A Green Rose Book

New Issues Poetry & Prose
The College of Arts and Sciences
Western Michigan University
Kalamazoo, Michigan 49008

First Edition, 2002.

ISBN   1-930974-14-0 (paperbound)

Library of Congress Cataloging-in-Publication Data:
Hogue, Cynthia
Flux/Cynthia Hogue
Library of Congress Control Number: 2001132691

Art Direction   Joseph Wingard
Design   Matthew Travis
Production   Paul Sizer
                  The Design Center, Department of Art
                  College of Fine Arts
                  Western Michigan University
Printing   Courier Corporation

Flux

Cynthia Hogue

New Issues

WESTERN MICHIGAN UNIVERSITY

Also by Cynthia Hogue

The Never Wife
The Woman in Red
Where the Parallels Cross
Touchwood
Scheming Women: Poetry, Privilege, and the Politics of Subjectivity

Books edited by Cynthia Hogue:

*We Who Love To Be Astonished: Experimental Women's Writing
and Performance Poetics* (co-edited with Laura Hinton)

In memory of Knud-Erik Holme Pedersen,
Ian Fletcher, Sheila Zamora, and Naiya Treybich

Contents

I.

What Is Given You

Questions like Indian summer,
like shale, the layers pressing down
until they form into the new-
hued purpose of marble,
the color of dead leaves
or of those who look back.

It is better to look
at the black line of hills
against the night.
A child's gift—the crow, found
in the yard, brought to mother
who burns it.
Not before the child discovers
pale flecks moving
through its coat: a smell
webbed with cheeping from the nest
she finds in the pine next day.
She follows the sound to the very top,
sticks her hands in a softness
of fledglings. Two

will fall out during the night,
another will die from cold, and the last
will be crushed in her hand
as she tries to bring it safely down—
the blood streaks around her eyes
when she rubs them:

like an ancient charm
for waning until she's the darker flecks
of blackberries, the seeds
a crow will pick and bear home,
to her own.

The Message

Gongs in white surplices, beshrouded wails
Far strum of fog horns . . . signals dispersed in veils.
                                    —Hart Crane

We wait for something to change.
Weather hovers like a circling
red-tipped hawk. And leaves,
not flaming, fall and hide
the mouse sniffing in dry grass.

Below us, fog veils city and bay,
dispersing the signals
of ghosts sailing masts to sea.

When we look up—migrating pigeons,
wind and the sun's steady confrontation—
a deer on the hill's crest
dances and stills. A messenger, but who's
to teach us that language?

The Book of Years

Mishearing the sentence when a storm rose
off the horizon like a bad habit,
muttering chaos, meaningless,
we drove through a scourge of hail.

We wished to feel airy, scooped-out.
Uncertain of what to do, we wanted
a *lift* as sensible and sublime
as moonflowers in the night air:

the solution to bloom so richly
that it distilled content,
gathering small losses
like a bouquet—the indigos, violets,

pinks laced with baby's breath,
forget-me-nots. We wake,
shaken, to cold, each
other, a surfeit.

Outside our ken,
the ice-locked oak
leaves shatter
in language's bitter winds.

It Isn't Raining

On her porch, the woman shakes
her umbrella twice as if
at the fevered man walking by
on his way to give his daily sermon
in the town square. She's left the blue-

and-lilied umbrella all over town,
like a crutch she couldn't use.
The man preaches in an elegantly-
lined raincoat, summers and winters,
his nose red in February, purple by March.

He brings news
to the ignorant, the blind
or fearless, of the coming
conflagration, then hitches home
with his brown bag full

of still-to-be-saved souls.
Not unlike the man's, the woman's words
bud cryptograms—aromatic code
to quell need. The sky
is a door she can open.

Storm Versions

If you're caught in a storm
make a hollow from snow.
Keep close to your center,
hands under armpits,
your body a cocoon.

       I've heard the soul
       wastes its time. But in storms
       it gathers, rooting, sturdy.

Skiers find you in the mound
that kept you.
Their dogs have brandy
but don't drink it. Now
that you're too heavy for houses

       you lie down.
       Then like those in cars,
       those stranded shrouds

you emerge in spring,
soggy with run-off, your shell
discarded, wriggled out of...

       You don't wake up.
       You're never found.
       You're mulch for seed.

Or what was inside:
glistening like the just-
born that sunned dry
and flicked its tail,
tunneled down through clay,

       brown and wet, leaving a space
       the breadth of bone.

Covering Tracks

I walked in a cold place over ice
and my lover skied ahead with the dogs
getting in his way:

My eyes were ringed like an owl
who has watched all night
for the skinny winter squirrel. But hunter,

you came instead, thought him
a deer you'd lucked into,
routed him deeper into woods.
I followed the spotty trail he left,
found him covered lightly with snow.

Now there's no rest—
"Don't go back," he said,
but I've got you
threaded into the seam the brain makes
between what you admit
and what you won't.

I'll tell you: It has already come
to blows. Your hand
yanked the hair back
from my scalp,
your fist through the particle
board wall punched an opening
you wished was my face.
I watched your kids
coming and going, drunk, shivering,
spewing foam at each other.

I don't want to see
them anymore and I don't want
to write you: I draw circles
and curses in a glitter
I wish was uranium.
I've sprinkled it all over
your wife, through the hole in the wall,
and on your peaceful napping,
until nightfall
            gives at its seams.

The Sense of Being Watched by More than
We Can See

after a line by Wendell Berry

The twig twists and humps
like a crippled child
who has died.
It draws to a point
branching into a hand.
I crouch, we shake:

Crouching taught you to listen.
You pricked your ears back,
and heard better,
tried snow falling on a twig.
Tried your ear on tracks
you've learned to read.

But you left that peace
when I came back. We drift
through layers of air   hot and cold
like currents in a body
like water   ghosts
weaving around trees   graying
into dusk.

How many times before
I saw the first gravestone?
(Like noticing deer
from the road   counting them
and as your eyes adjust
finding more and more.)
Standing awry   cracked   rain-
stained, some still shaded by a tree (older).

And the mending wall
built with stones cleared
from the field whose last crop
is a forgotten thing,
like the graves of children
who died in one sweep.

The Valley between the Pigeon and Panther Mountains

Facets

Rain billowed the curtains
like a sleepwalker's arms.
What did you say?
Two people in another room—
She covers a gift with her hand;
his rests against it.
But you said something?
The lake rises an inch.
There's no one
to answer.

~

She has driven away—
is watching the trees'
inner moves.
Light is temperamental
in late summer storms,
when edges gone with heat
suck it up
as lichen, moisture.
Human
moves: her desire
for grace.

~

The cat wants out.
You do not budge.
You moan in your sleep.
Is it bad, what you wake to
soaked through each morning?
The cat then
wants in.

~

Children are steaming in sleep.
I can see smoke rising next door.
But the scent of yeast?
Their shapes risen
in summer houses.

Something to do with the symmetry
of green. Unconscious,
agile as minnows.

~

Whether she trusts him
is a matter of preference.
She forgets the lake was once
three ponds, hallowed.
Before they vanished
its people moved off to the valley
between the Pigeon and Panther Mountains.
Their shadows were stolen.
Their bones burrowed down caverns
which give passing hunters
the sudden jitters:

As this man who is so tired
of this business with a woman
who sits on a rock by water
watching the green lichen
increase into coils.

The Way to the Lake

Was lost this fall.
We knew we'd find it again,
familiar path through woods.
The landmarks:
great oak struck by lightning
(a hole through its heart)—
the lichened rock we called sacred
at the water's edge.

But this time
everything was wrong.
The oak had surely been *there*,
the rock far too small for us
to sit and watch how weather
transforms water.
But worse was the lake—
shriveled pond by a sawmill
turning to marshland.

Crying *no* as one,
we flailed around in the forest
until lost, we said we'd lost the lake.
Now I think that we'll build
a shelter out of leaves,
try tomorrow with first light.
It won't do to lose hope.
But the others say, Let's
get the hell out of here.
Not another minute, we won't stay
another minute in this place.

The Gathering Beyond Fog

A large encampment, all women
giving birth:
I search for clean cloth
and bring boiling water
to midwives. Somehow
I should know what else to do

but, uninitiated,
I find a dress for one
whose after-birth won't drop.
The child's soul
in danger. It wants to follow
the mother who has refused
further help. The baby

folds with first pain—
smells of ginger and sweet basil,
but when I look, its genitals
are hidden. Outside the camp,

trees sconced in fog.
If I could see in,
the forms of a different
matter would be visible: the after-
death we've been trying to bring

to that level
of mist. A silhouette
whose vaporous edge
nurses the child, fog which is slowly
descending on women

in a newly formed circle. We are all
cold, moving
closer. If there's longing
for men we've forgotten.
Like pain, the fog has no ceiling.

After the Great Rain

We tried remembering
about roots, mushrooms—all over
the place, but which ones?
Leaves, feces, fire

made from damp wood.
We breathed that smoke
as if it would bring back the dead.
Left emptied, our hands

fumbled for the braille
of runes chiseled on rocks
wedged like markers
in crevices high above the water line.

You came for me in sleep
prodding me with your stories:
listen for crows
when they reel from the branches

of crowned birch. Their calls
lead you to hidden fields
of berries just ripe. Cross
with salamanders the long breast

of road in darkness. Gold stripes
rippling down their backs
turn incandescent, smoldering
with the force of birth.

It may take everything you have
to reach for that.
Though I knew next morning
we would not make it through.

Edging Winter

Leaden as fish under ice,
carp in small lakes,
we stay small:
the landscape's reduced
to snow we can't see through.
We shade our eyes.

To move it
we find the lynx and snow rabbit—
tracks conjured the night before—
mark the trail with bits of metal,
strap wood to boots and glide through
take the same route back—it's easy
to sink, to lose the way.

And if a hand and a cigarette
caught at a right angle against light
make a cross on the face across the table,
I cry out
as if I'd prayed
for your safe-keeping through storm.

Like the lynx
in a forest, a certain
faith hovers near me—
only its eyes at night.
Sometimes a choking sound.

But one morning
ice on the whole lake
breaks all at once and heaves into peace:
a sound we're given to ex-
tend ourselves
out from this frozen time.

Like carp in spring creeks
we grow sleek again,
bony and inedible.
Vague shapes wave to us,
but who? We're moving

toward that dark line
where ice clears shore
and breaks for sea.

Signs

Birds in the house.
An owl is shot by the front door.
An old midwife talks to herself.

The oak, its trunk branching
then braided back, a hole there
like the giant eye of a needle.
You're the thread to go through.
If you climb up, you could sew
some leaves back on.

Your grandmother visits you
in dreams, tells you what comes true—
one bad, one good. She threatens
never to speak again
because you don't want to see
the future when it's given you:
Please, no more, no more.

You're on your knees
but it's been a long time—
you can't remember the words.
You flash a mirror into the clearing.

The report of a gun,
and an owl falls by the door.
You hang it head down from a beam.
All winter it'll drain and bleach,

the tiny bones dissolving. Nothing
but skin by spring, the eyes hard
dark clouds, the beak half-open,
and the claws *still sharp for rain.*

II.

The Insatiate

Beak full-tilt to the wind,
a crow caws nearby: magenta tulip
opens an inner dusty gold
to the January sun
whose colors over the sea
are the same hues washed on cirrus.

I hadn't noticed the bird
or flower braving winter until now,
nor the odor of boiling meat
pungent through the house,
broth for someone's soup.
For days I've listened to no music.

The wind insists, tireless and hollow
around these third floor rooms.
And the sea at the earth-wall,
trespasser by night. Maybe
it is this broth that
has me squeezing past the tulip

through the window ajar for air,
hair swept to feathers
before a gray weather front
that breaches shore.

The Wandering of the Soul

It is when she is so quiet,
the moon waning to its crescent,
two arguments, almost a third,
and impulses curdled to *self*.
She's empty enough to leave
body and trudge out
into snow
       though it started before snow.

The first stirrings, a glimpse
of cliff crags, viscous moors,
their lava flowing into stone,
and boulders gathered near mounds
where fish hang from scaffolds on the coast

to dry, fish heads in bundles
headed for Africa as delicacy.
Cold grayness. The shore of traces:
refuse from the Westman Islands, driftwood
from Siberia, stone foundlings of farm
and sheep pen, beheaded seal

she steps on, gingerly pressing
her foot down, up,
as if there's still breath in him.
She squats, looking for life in tide pools,
sand and kelp in muted drift-patterns.
Empty shells. The drive back
in a silence speckled with words.

First flakes hit the windshield,
no lights around the city up ahead.
She has waited for this element
that mutes even the road before her.

The Changeling

*after an Icelandic folktale in which an elf child
is exchanged for a human one*

Loftur. His name means air,
and my cries
wend up to him,
floating
on the currents
of afterbirth, the veil

of second sight
still wrapped around his head.
You mean wind.
Husband, I know what I named him.
He witnessed his own birth;
it caught his breath

like a raven swooping to catch a berry
as it drops from the bush.
When a cold front moved off sea,
to the ring of mountains—
everything gave way to stillness
I could not escape.

His first impulse was flight
out from under this lid
toward another vision,
but was he blind to the one we have?
*You mean storm, brewing around us,
had he waited to ride it out?*

I mean this child left to me, without cowl,
breath gone from him,
no cry issued,
nothing for me to nurture.
By now he's back there,
knew where to go—

his hand extended to grasp
the forerunner's, and when they touch,
all the dark feathered beings will rivet
the air with their calls and I'll
shudder through root and stone.
You mean rain

will come soon.
This time, I will follow.
They are brothers now
someone else must raise.

Tracks of Sound and Water

A boy spends seven years painting clouds,
learning to read what they tell.
Finally, his paintings become sky.

    Here, a mist of sulfur
    rises off the bay.
    No trees to hide me
    from the distant glacier,
    the salmon sun
    singeing horizon, the wind burning.

He spends seven years learning the uses
of plants—eucalyptus, chamomile, nettle—
names that he can hear the wind in,
as when he gathered them
from hills, desert, and woods.

Seven years healing,
until he's alert
as a deer in open field.
Always he's preparing
for a dream someone else would have.

    How long did I look,
    at last calling myself back?
    Through amber fumes steeping up,
    the bay smoking, mountains in clouds.

An eagle tries to catch a dolphin
for so many years he understands at last
the creature's laughing.
The dreamer says, *When you hear that*
from one in human form
you'll see cloud leaf root water—
as sound—and the joy in that
will fool you.

I heard chants.
Five times at the mountain's foot
near the corpse-stones,
I was dipped in the well,
once for each note of the scale.

The dreamer's eyes narrow
until the boy sees only
black pupil, is thrown
to the ground.
There are three tasks left.
The first is to discover the other two.
When you know the second,
become the third.

I knew I was a dream as well,
not looking, through fine mist,
but there, with the wings
I had need of.

A raven starts from the bush,
flies up, cawing.
The sound stays with the boy's body for years.
The dreamer says, *I leave you with this:*
when you've fulfilled the last,
it is fire, not air,
you'll gather.

Where is there left to look?
And this evening, when the wind dies
and the sun drops from the clouds...

The boy cannot tell whether it's song
or the peal of laughter around and inside him.
The sound becomes a trail
he follows to the water's edge,
wades in, then swims out—
at times leaping airborn—
into the flickering tracks of light.

The Sorcerer

Near the graves of the great dead,
Even the stones speak.
                    —Theodore Roethke

No one could control him,
the smallest of the clan.
        The leaves shiver as we pass through
        the hedge, out from shelter.
        A branch snaps.
At school he was always up to something,
screwed a girl in the back room at 14,
then opened a door in the wall,
led her in, but his powers
couldn't keep the door open.

Years later, her skeleton found
upright, the fetal bones poised inside.
No one asked questions.
        The wind shoves
        up into our jackets, whips scarf
        against skin, and two horses in distance,
        one riderless, the other becoming one
        with his rider, gallop into sleet.

His power grown beyond the living,
he turned to the dead.
In the belfry, one by one,
all the ancient practitioners
rose to his chant:
until one whose book,
buried with him, could open to the boy
the threshold he wanted to cross. And almost
he touched that fragile vellum.

Then birds startled from the tower,
bells chimed his dream until he saw
his hand reaching into dust-filled air. And whispered
near his head: *Doomed one, how you were close
to owning my book.*
        And how we pull and pull our limbs
        through an oblivion of snow.

after an Icelandic folktale

Portals

Midnight. A cold sweat past season.
By May, dawn breaks the dark continuum.
But not until four. Now is for swans
in flight, their calls a sonar telling

where they are, how they keep formation.
In the light from Northern House I see them
fly low past a stand of scrub birch
that bud a chartreuse easing into spring:

like sleep's easy drift until tremors of sound
flecked the dark, and wide awake,
I saw a light
that shuttered the stars, the sky

split across and sprung
from its center wings
children make in snow.

Though what it was
was not snow, but like vapor exhaled, inhaled,
contracting. Gone then.

But my senses wring
from unsalvaged night—a swan's passage
down the wind. It's that journey I want now,
into fathomless white.

The Strange Land

*I asked about ruins . . . 'No stranger has seen them, and
. . . nobody tramps around without me knowing it.'*
    —From Helge Ingstad's conversation with the caretaker
    on the site of the first Viking settlement in Vinland

There, sunlight in winter
was a pale wash for whose color
some child drew breath: the bearing
of blue to her lungs: her eyes
stared defiantly back.
She took great pains

training a crow to sit on her arm.
He has learned three words
but just as I listen hard
they garble: his claws
rake her skin and she curses
the doctor stitching
with his needle too soon.
But to the bird she calls
Here I am; where are you?

It's perched on a branch
by the window. From that spot,
my memory of willows
exactly the same and utterly different:

take a beach, what was cleared to make it
grown up again, the landmarks,
invisible. What is abiding

is aberrant, a joke
grandmother told the child
who has her own version of how
the peasants of Thule
made a soup so thin
the peas called back and forth,
Here I am; where are you?

In another place. Not a lake.
Nor parched tongue of valley
below the Superstitions. Where I
compose myself again. Somewhere
that may last until peace
funnels through a rusty spiral
clear up to cumulus

which hold their breath
past the mountains,
past summer and the climb
through early darkness in winter.

Who asked of excavations,
of ruin? Who came and left first,
with a wind off the strange land?

III.

At the End of Things

The air cleared after the Santa Anas
blew through leaving a trail
of migraines, downed eucaplytus seeds,
and suicides. We had drinks
on the hillside patio, could see across the valley
to mountains usually sconced in smog,

now scored by light, numbed to it.
A coyote ambled across the road
looking for a cat or small dog.
Sleek and smart. A survivor, I thought.
I hid even from myself my bitter heart.
Evening searched for us.

I looked between the lights,
my eyes no longer seeing.
Some called it blindness.
There was no right or wrong
I had not dreamed, though the soul
has bandaged moments.

Write or Die

after H.D.

She sees her breath before her.
If I could stir, she thinks,
and she can. She rises
like a tall fir, green, blue
(there's a ghost—white
on white—hovering on the periphery).
Write *or die*? Did someone
say, We rise again

from pain and *love*, to her?
Or is she *not-self* at the sea?
Soul-smoldering, burgeoning?

Water sputters with light
as snow speckles the dark
autumn hills. Steely bars
mar the sunset, scratched across
a salmony sky. The coast,
with its shagged, eroded cliffs and rock-
strewn crags, reminds her of something,
something she's lost words for.

Gratitude Is the Only Secret
That Cannot Reveal Itself

after Emily Dickinson

When Time stopped, she wrote on sky-
colored paper, *for the Crocus*
(Glory flooded the garden) . . .
"My father taught me time but
I did not understand & was afraid."
Her life, aslant as March buds
in late frost, grief for ballast.

Water boiled, windows
scrubbed of winter-smudge.
A town, gray as Eternity.
Then "step like a pattering child's and in
glided a little plain woman
with no good feature, who said,
'Forgive me; I never see strangers.'"

She smiled (though she never smiled),
breathless. Air nodded, entranced.
"If I ask too much, please refuse.
I find ecstasy in living
and shortness to live
makes me bold." Breeze arose
to recall Loss striding forty days

through the valley, hands clasped behind,
wing-shadows hovering overhead.
She thought to plead
for affection, but "what is Affection
but the Germ of little Notes?"
(This *very* dreamily, as if they were comets
she writes.) Wind pulled

its lace shawl close, tittered.
"Is it oblivion or absorption
when things pass from our minds?
I have'nt expressed myself
strongly enough." Silence paused
as just beyond the pane
a robin quipped in green.

The Waterfall

In another time,
my husband would teach me
to fish the pool
this rushing water
fills. In fact, he's
farther upstream
teaching our son,

never born, both shadows in a light
that falls through spruce.

They cannot see how I dive
beyond rock underneath.
What I find there are intrusions
of quartz designed
to hide the way back.
I pull at a stone,
then everything shifts

to reveal the bison
curving its neck
to lick fur, a leaping
antelope, or a woman kneeling
for a bath or prayer—all of this
jeweled with agate and jasper.

My husband looks down into water,
his eyes couched and dark.
He knows that separate,
we grow. If I were to rise
like a geyser from the pool's
smooth granite bed, even then

to couple in a place
formed thousands of years ago,
yet would I be thunder
of falling water, a thirst
increased, and unquenched.

Like Exile

for my mother

From the porch I hear metal
clang with the resonance
of a bell rung in my grandfather's old church
the moment he died. They say the wind
caused it, for it was far
late in the night.
Lilacs circling the grounds
heard. The ancient specters
of pear, cherry, and plum trees
behind the parsonage heard.
And those whose sacrament
he'd read. I heard by the ringing
of our phone, ran upstairs
to cover my head. At that moment,
his daughter was on a train.
Now she writes of the closing
words to the evening,
May He make His face to shine...
      as the bulb of cactus
      whose natal web of fibers
      shrouds needles too soft
      to be plucked for any sound
with grace unto you...
      upon the ledge of shale
      I've climbed to
      watch the hills russet,
      their edges hazy before dusk
      sinks their light into my arms
      even to that horizon
like sound's travel—this bell—
accident or anger of some workman
I've run out to meet.
No one in sight. I try finding my hands;
they're too smooth, pale.

My ears ring. I forget
everything, nothing.
Mother looks back and
her face is her father's. That vision
merges with desert heat in this city
where I line yellow palo verde flowers
upon an unused bridge
and listen for the hour's chiming
from a belfry whose shadow is luminous
like those never-to-wake unborn
my body is too marred to bear.

The Delicate Webbing

A rope frayed to breaking.
Your steps overhead. A swelling
in the clitoris, burned to earth-shadows
by a secret witness. Scent of orange.

> Grandmother waited six years
> for her chosen husband. Grew quiet,
> talked to herself. Then he came,
> picked her up, just like that...

> Twenty years after he died,
> she thinks of him kindly,
> skin taut on cheekbones,
> eyes of the Lapland
> wolf, that stoic
> grace.
>   She clacks
> her dentures into place.

I fidget in my seat.
Dreams can be useful, safe;
they travel the wind like hawks.

Those I love have no patience.
They look past me. When I sleep
the west wind curves under the window,
circles our bed, the mind
mulling this last question.

The Light at Our Backs

for R.L.

Adobe walls. No north side to the house.
Could be no roof: someone has painted
the ceiling blue with clouds.
The wind changes direction.
I lick a finger, but can't tell
which way. It's around and inside me.
I take off my clothes.

Now you see a thin-veined body,
as insistent as a woman listening,
but for what? A lake
trapped through canyon? Cliffs
mottled with chartreuse, rust, and black lichen?
A mockingbird on a reed-like branch?
You wait to see the white
spread of underwing through air.

We climb further,
where barbed wire startles
the length of the ridge.
When I turn to say *That's where
we'll go*, you're nowhere in sight.
The wind is up fourfold. But the water
at last become night's eye,
catches a glimmering house
rising at my back.

Inside, a chair breathes
as if someone had gotten up
and was walking through the whitest rooms.
You can't move or speak,
though were you to look now
you'd see an unsettling
light blooming into mouth,
at the edge, where a wall
used to be.

The Blue-Shadowed Canyon

> *Rose, cobalt-violet, cadmium*
> *pressed into buttes, positioned guards*
> *at whose feet alluvial mounds*
> *sink like boots in the Colorado*
> *scraping relentlessly...*
> —after Cassandra

I was taken from the rubble.
Who should have none,
have this man. It is not
the first night: he is home.
I've watched the half-moon
rise between juniper branches.

In the first light, clouds were like a veil.
I watched them turn from the color
of the cougar's tongue
to the color of its underbelly,
slit gutted then pulled over four poles
that my husband walks under.
There are drops on his face.

I tell him crows, shard-bone
hawks, flies—what hovers.
I said it many times.
You can hear them outside.
I screamed in his face
because the whites under his irises
rolled up. His belly-
laugh when I begged that we go
to his bath. Now over-
cast, the distance, a huge lake.

Shadows on the plain.
Stop your sparrow chatter.
The lake is stained
the hue of dawn.
I head out for it,
wailing so the deaf
know where I am.

Finding the Way Back

My husband calls me *little salamander*,
tells me what herbs to chew for sleep.
I won't remember the names next day—
try juniper berries, goldenseal,
the flaming witches' hair, its fibers
hooked over the spine of amaranth branches
until they collapse. Yesterday he fell,
must use a cedar branch I smoothed with sand.

We stop often—our hoods pulled low
against dust, the ties whipping in wind.
One snaps against my cheek
leaving a mark that pulses all evening.
I rub it with salve
he pulls from his sack.

A lizard drops its tail.
He says she'll grow another—
this one's for us.
He takes his crutch
and a long thigh bone,
pitches tent with his cloak.
Mine wraps us barely,
pear-shaped, hunched close.
This time I don't sleep.

In the morning we suck water
distilled in a small hole
we covered last night.
Swish it on my tongue
for as long as I can.

My husband says we'll enter the canyon
for shelter tonight, find the darker line
where mud runs like a new layer
along its wall. He says we won't
need water, that we'll cup
our hands *under the clouds*.

Interior

for S.Z. (1947-1978)

It is not the confined space
of hospitals—the walls that angle in
to where you're still ringed with vessels
gone to the ice-white of your skin.
My sister had just walked in to check.
She is wrapping you
in the sheet. Another
helps her swing you to a roll-away.
The window spreads fingers
against the breaking
light. A pale almond
disrupts the sky's gray. You
are the third in two days.

> She says *Enough.*
> *I will care for the old.*
> *Is it really so late?*

I make breath
marks on my own clean glass.
When I turn at the sound of a voice
my sister is staring with your eyes.
I cannot see one tree from where I am,
one leaf, just the fence
only the cat climbs with ease.

We make more of ourselves in early
spring, we're all so ready
to appease the winter hound.
While I drove up through the mountains
of Taos and slept in a triangle made
by trees, the magnetic grid of that grove
through which you rose
was yellow and riddled
as if you'd stepped
for a moment behind a stand of creosote:

You were in flight. So long ago
that another death has come between,
and *hers* becomes *yours?*

This is not the room
lit with fluorescents.
Outside, heat lightning brings
no more than itself to bear
down like a hoarse mew that heaves back
to some murky corner and smolders...
or in a large nightly file that drags past.

Periwinkle, wheat—the names that surface,
your flower, your grain, your birth-
right: you didn't intend
that you would lie flat, body
immaterial, the woman of you
harbored in our scrawls,
or the relentless convergence of bells.

Flux

The shade's pulled. Behind it
the lake has no tide.

    When you want to fuse two things together
    they have to be clean   pure   solid.

The room's empty.
My husband's scent hovers like smoke.
I dream he's been away,
all these years to leave.
I must see him before he dies.

    You use flux: cleans the metal,
    also   joins and lets the solder work.

Then I do. He's purged.
Mourners file past,
tears rubbed into his skin,
then mine.

    Flux: white crystals,
    like salt: you mix it with water
    sprinkle it
    throw it over your shoulder
    give it to a woman
    who has stopped flowing.

I place two shiny metal pieces
on each eye. The bone of brow
showing through vexes him:
let the dead rest and don't try
to bring me back either now I'm gone.

    Flux changes the element
    you work in. *Husband*
    solder   earth   air

Agape

He emerged from the cave
as from grief. Her waiting
done, the woman gaped. Timely,

she saw how he lay
in a full field, wrapped
still in the winding sheet,

bodied forth. He was buried
but arose; she wrote, burying
herself in words, apocryphal,

unheeded. The man had erred
truly, whether he spoke—
as she said, one last message:

"I like order, things
that go according to plan.
You bring chaos"—

or not. Day one: isolation.
Day two: morbidity. Day three:
he'd think of this change

as peaceful, just walking
on air like earth. She'd
disappear, who stood agape

as clouds changed from dove
to mauve, the sun
a lucent disk above

the hills broken by rose
buttes. And in silhouette,
a soaring hawk.

Notes

"Gratitude Is the Only Secret That Cannot Reveal Itself": Quoted passages are from Letters 342 and 342b, 16 August, 1870, Col. Higginson to his wife, on meeting Emily Dickinson for the first time; Letter 352, 26 September, 1870, Dickinson to Col. Higginson.

"Write or Die": Quoted passages are from H.D.'s *Hermetic Definition*.

Acknowledgments

Grateful acknowledgment is made to the editors of the journals in which some of these poems first appeared, some in earlier versions:

Alaska Quarterly Review: "Flux," "Storm Versions"

Connecticut Review: "The Insatiate," "The Waterfall"

Cutbank: "After the Great Rain," "Signs"

Greenfield Review: "The Sense of Being Watched by More than We Can See," "Finding the Way Back"

Ice Floe: "The Sorcerer," "The Wandering of the Soul"

In Posse: "Like Exile," "Gratitude Is the Only Secret That Cannot Reveal Itself"

Many Mountains Moving: "Tracks of Sound and Water"

New Orleans Review: "Write or Die," "Agape"

Passages North: "The Gathering Beyond Fog"

Porch: "Portals"

Quarterly West: "The Message"

Raccoon: "Covering Tracks"

Red Rock Review: "The Book of Years," "At the End of Things," "It Isn't Raining"

Seneca Review: "What Is Given You," "Edging Winter"

Willow Springs: "Interior"

Some of these poems first appeared in the original Inland Boat series of chapbooks, published by *Porch,* under the title *Touchwood.* Others were originally published as a limited edition chapbook in England, under the title *Where the Parallels Cross* (Whiteknights Press). "The Gathering Beyond Fog" was included in *The Passages North Anthology.*

I am grateful to the United States Educational Foundation in Iceland, whose Fulbright Fellowship made it possible for me to write some of these poems, and to Herbert Scott, for his careful and exacting editing of this collection, as well as for his encouragement at a crucial time. Abiding thanks to Norman Dubie and Ian Fletcher for their early help and support, as well as to Pamela Stewart, Dean Stover, Jeanne Clarke, Kirpal Gordon, Deirdre O'Connor, Adrian Oktenberg, Karl Patten, Peggy Shumaker, and Stacey Waite for friendship and feedback through the years.

photo by Jan Pearson

Cynthia Hogue has published three collections of poetry, most recently *The Never Wife* (Mammoth Press, 1999), and has co-edited an anthology of essays on women's avant-garde writing, *We Who Love To Be Astonished: Experimental Women's Writing and Performance Poetics* (University of Alabama Press, 2001). For her work, she has received NEA, NEH, and Fulbright fellowships. She is a trained mediator specializing in diversity issues in education. She has lived and taught in Iceland, Arizona, New Orleans, and New York. She currently lives in Pennsylvania, where she directs the Stadler Center for Poetry and teaches English at Bucknell University.

New Issues Poetry & Prose

Editor, Herbert Scott

James Armstrong, *Monument in a Summer Hat*
Michael Burkard, *Pennsylvania Collection Agency*
Anthony Butts, *Fifth Season*
Kevin Cantwell, *Something Black in the Green Part of Your Eye*
Gladys Cardiff, *A Bare Unpainted Table*
Kevin Clark, *In the Evening of No Warning*
Jim Daniels, *Night with Drive-By Shooting Stars*
Joseph Featherstone, *Brace's Cove*
Lisa Fishman, *The Deep Heart's Core Is a Suitcase*
Robert Grunst, *The Smallest Bird in North America*
Mark Halperin, *Time as Distance*
Myronn Hardy, *Approaching the Center*
Edward Haworth Hoeppner, *Rain Through High Windows*
Cynthia Hogue, *Flux*
Janet Kauffman, *Rot* (fiction)
Josie Kearns, *New Numbers*
Maurice Kilwein Guevara, *Autobiography of So-and-so: Poems in Prose*
Ruth Ellen Kocher, *When the Moon Knows You're Wandering*
Steve Langan, *Freezing*
Lance Larsen, *Erasable Walls*
David Dodd Lee, *Downsides of Fish Culture*
Deanne Lundin, *The Ginseng Hunter's Notebook*
Joy Manesiotis, *They Sing to Her Bones*
Sarah Mangold, *Household Mechanics*
David Marlatt, *A Hog Slaughtering Woman*
Paula McLain, *Less of Her*
Sarah Messer, *Bandit Letters*
Malena Mörling, *Ocean Avenue*
Julie Moulds, *The Woman with a Cubed Head*
Marsha de la O, *Black Hope*
C. Mikal Oness, *Water Becomes Bone*
Elizabeth Powell, *The Republic of Self*
Margaret Rabb, *Granite Dives*
Rebecca Reynolds, *Daughter of the Hangnail*
Martha Rhodes, *Perfect Disappearance*
Beth Roberts, *Brief Moral History in Blue*
John Rybicki, *Traveling at High Speeds*

Mary Ann Samyn, *Inside the Yellow Dress*
Mark Scott, *Tactile Values*
Martha Serpas, *Côte Blanche*
Diane Seuss-Brakeman, *It Blows You Hollow*
Marc Sheehan, *Greatest Hits*
Sarah Jane Smith, *No Thanks—and Other Stories* (fiction)
Phillip Sterling, *Mutual Shores*
Angela Sorby, *Distance Learning*
Russell Thorburn, *Approximate Desire*
Robert VanderMolen, *Breath*
Martin Walls, *Small Human Detail in Care of National Trust*
Patricia Jabbeh Wesley, *Before the Palm Could Bloom: Poems of Africa*